First-class zulu 'Celandine' BF737 crossing the bar into Great Yarmouth on a windy day, c.1895. The large size of the vessel in relation to her crew is clear, yet she is still being tossed about by the waves. Behind her is a fifie from Eyemouth. The strength of the wind can be seen in the way the sail is pulling away from the yard, which itself is bending.

C000186501

SCOTTISH FISHING BOATS

Matthew Tanner

Shire Publications Ltd

CONTENTS

Published in 1996 by Shire Publications Ltd, Cromwell House, Church Street, Princes Risborough, Buckinghamshire HP27 9AA, UK. Copyright © 1996 by Matthew Tanner. First published 1996. Shire Album 326. ISBN 0 7478 0317 X.

Matthew Tanner is hereby identified as the author of this work in accordance with Section 77 of the Copyright, Designs and Patents Act 1988.

All rights reserved. No part of this publication may be reproduced or transmitted in any form or by any means, electronic or mechanical, including photocopy, recording, or any information storage and retrieval system, without permission in writing from the publishers.

Printed in Great Britain by CIT Printing Services, Press Buildings, Merlins Bridge, Haverfordwest, Dyfed SA61 1XF.

British Library Cataloguing in Publication Data: Tanner, Matthew. Scottish Fishing Boats. – (Shire Album: 326). 1. Fishing boats – Scotland – History. I. Title. 387. 2'0426'09411. ISBN 0-7478-0317-X.

ACKNOWLEDGEMENTS

The photograph of the Viking boat (page 3) is reproduced by courtesy of the Viking Ship Museum, Roskilde, Denmark. All other photographs, including the cover, are by courtesy of the Scottish Fisheries Museum and the assistance of the Director and staff of the museum is gratefully acknowledged.

Cover: *The restored 72 foot (22 metre) fifie 'Reaper' FR958 operated by the Scottish Fisheries Museum.*

Below: *A Scottish salmon coble (pronounced 'cobble') setting off to work at Montrose, c.1910. The three men are going out to tend the fixed salmon 'stake' net which can be dimly seen in the background. The characteristics of the coble are clearly seen. She has a very broad platform for carrying nets at the stern, and a strong uplift to the bow to aid launching and handling in the broken waters of the beach areas where she works.*

A probable Viking fishing boat. This is the Skuldelev six-oar boat dating from about AD 1000 and recovered in 1962 from the bottom of Roskilde Fjord in Denmark. She is now displayed in a support frame at the Viking Ship Museum, Roskilde, where the clinker construction with light frames and high flared ends is easily seen.

EARLY DAYS AND THE NORTHERN ISLES

Viking raiding ships sailed the North Sea to pillage and settle the fertile lands of Orkney, Shetland and the Hebrides from the end of the eighth century AD. Shetland did not become part of Scotland until 1469, and it is there that the closest parallels can be found between Scottish boats and Viking craft. Much attention has been given to the great Viking warrior longships but examples of their smaller vessels and fishing boats have been discovered too.

Viking and Shetland boats were clinker-built and double-ended, with generally wide planks. Most remarkably, the light frames were not fastened to the keel but only to the planks, allowing the boat structure to flex and move with the waves. Clinker construction consists of overlapping planks which are joined at the edges.

3

Clinker boats are usually built 'shell first' and small stiffeners are built inside after the hull is finished. The resulting boat is strong but lightweight and requires little caulking. There is virtually no indigenous supply of wood in Shetland and so the raw materials for boats were regularly imported from Norway, often prepared in kit form.

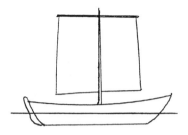

Sixern, c.36 feet (10.9 metres).

Fair Isle skiff, c.20 feet (6.1 metres).

The *Fair Isle skiff* and *Dunrossness yole* (from south Shetland) were probably closest to their Viking forebears. They were undecked rowing and sailing boats that were ideally suited to hand lining for the abundant fish around the voes and skerries of the islands. Only they could survive and work in an area of notorious tides, whirlpools and short steep breaking seas where boats had to be agile and light. The high flared stem and stern helped keep the broken water out and held plenty of reserve buoyancy, while the short keel and marked sheer and the ease of moving them under oar enabled them to react easily and quickly to the irregular waves. A mast of roughly the same length as the keel was stepped slightly forward of amidships. Fair Isle was one of the last places to use a traditional Viking-style square sail.

In the eighteenth and nineteenth centuries many boats known as *fourerns* or *fourereens* and *sixerns* or *sixereens* were imported. These terms correspond closely with the Viking words for smaller boats: 'fourern' represents *færing*, meaning 'four-oars' and 'sixern' represents *sixæring*, meaning 'six-oars'. A complete Viking *færing* from the ninth century was uncovered inside the Gokstad ship burial in Oslo. The similarity with the Shetland fourern is striking although the fourern has a stern rudder and five or six plank

Yoles drawn up on the beach at Sandness, Shetland, c.1925. The broad plank runs and the strongly curving stem, stern and sheerline are quite distinctive.

Lerwick, Shetland, c.1900. In the foreground is a fourern and in the centre is a larger sixern. The mast is clearly stepped right in the middle of the boat and this indicates that she was probably using the traditional Viking-style square sail. The boat at the end of the jetty has her mast right forward and probably has a dipping lugsail rig.

An abandoned sixern lies rotting on the beach at Vemmentry, Shetland, in 1984. This boat may be the 34 foot (10.3 metre) 'Royal Exchange'.

The fishermen's memorial at Cullivoe, North Yell, Shetland, in 1993. The wife and child forever looking out to sea commemorate the disaster of July 1881 when fifty-eight fishermen were lost in nine sixerns and a small boat during a summer storm.

runs compared with the side-fastened rudder and three broad plank runs of the *færing*.

The great nineteenth-century sixerns represent the culmination of this strong Shetland Viking boat tradition. In the middle of the eighteenth century changes in the fish stocks on the rich Shetland fishing grounds forced the fishermen to head further offshore to seek cod and ling by long line. These changing circumstances required the old boats to change too and thus began the famous 'haaf' fishery. *Haaf* is the Norse word for 'ocean', for in this fishery the fishermen had to journey about 40 miles (64 km) out to sea, mostly under oar, to fish new grounds. It was said that the skylines of Norway in the east and Faroe in the west became quite familiar to them. The fishing lines had between one and two thousand baited hooks on them and stretched for 7 miles (11 km) on the seabed, taking up to eight hours to haul.

Sixerns were developed especially for this haaf fishery. They were big and fast open boats, up to 36 feet (10.9 metres) long, with curved stem and stern. Yet they were built in the lightweight Viking tradition so that they could still be worked off the beaches. Shetlanders rowed and sailed these craft far offshore in very dangerous waters and with no navigational aids other than their own experience. The skills required to navigate and ride out fierce storms in these open boats with square sails cannot be underestimated. Towards the end of the nineteenth century the traditional square sail was gradually replaced by the dipping lugsail rig which, although no easier to sail, provided better performance to windward.

In the latter years of the nineteenth century there was increasing contact with the Scottish mainland too, and the sixerns soon became neglected for the large potential profits of the herring fishery. Shetlanders invested quite heavily in the big herring luggers familiar in eastern Scotland, but they retained their smaller boats for inshore fishing, and today the fourern types are still used as maids of all work around the islands or close inshore at the 'eela' line-fishing for saithe. Fourerns are also popular racing sailing boats at Shetland regattas.

6

Launching the Hebridean sgoth 'Brothers Delight' SY148 from Tolsta beach, Lewis, in 1928. The size of these stout craft required a large number of men to move them down the beach. The strongly raked and rounded stern is quite apparent and the thole pins for the oars are easily seen along the top edge of the boat. The men of the crew are those wearing the long leather seaboots and in the foreground are the wooden baskets for the long fishing lines.

DEVELOPMENT ON THE WEST COAST

Most of the west coast of Scotland and the islands of the Hebrides never developed anything beyond a subsistence fishery. Despite the beautiful landscape, economic development was beset with difficulties, and small crofting communities were always struggling to stave off chronic poverty. The small boats that the crofters had were not capable of venturing out into the wide Minch where the herring shoals could be sought. Instead, they could take advantage only of the erratic arrival of a shoal within a sea loch close to home. Even then the difficulties of transport down the coast meant that a good catch might never find an economic market.

Only in Lewis did fishermen take up more commercial fishing. One of the most distinctive fishing-boat types is the Hebridean *sgoth* (pronounced 'scaw'). These stoutly built boats were used for line fishing from Lewis and Harris, and they had to be light enough to be operated from the open beaches but strong enough to withstand the pounding as they came ashore. They were double-ended sailing and rowing craft which show considerable development from their probable Viking fore-

bears. Although the stem had some curve in it like a sixern, they had a straight and raked sternpost under a very rounded stern and generous freeboard amidships which gave them a flat appearance with little sheer.

The very rounded, almost bowl-shaped stern is characteristic of many of the indigenous boats of the west coast. To build a round stern called for a high degree of boatbuilding skill, but the shape had plenty of buoyancy and made for a seaworthy craft. The round stern can be seen in old photographs of boats along the length of the coast. Even today many small boats can be found in the creeks,

Sgoth, c.25 feet (7.7 metres).

Loch Fyne skiffs lying at Campbeltown, c.1887. These three skiffs show all the characteristics of this common type. They have straight stems but raked sterns and the masts for the standing lugsails are stepped with a backward tilt.

usually in a derelict state, exhibiting this characteristic.

Loch Fyne and the lower Clyde area were more fortunate. A happy combination of fairly predictable herring shoals in relatively sheltered waters and, in Glasgow, the only large market on the coast allowed a full-time fishing industry to grow.

Drift-netting was the principal method employed in the early years of the nineteenth century, but in the 1830s a cheaper and more efficient method was developed, known as 'trawling'. This was the start of ring-netting and two distinct types of craft were developed to pursue it.

The first type was developed in the 1880s and became known as the *Loch* and

Loch Fyne skiff, c.30 feet (9.1 metres).

Fyne skiff. It was of similar size to the larger of the old-style skiffs, which had reached 30 feet (9.1 metres) in length, but the resemblance ended there. Loch Fyne skiffs had near-vertical stems and quite sharply raked and pointed sterns. The fore-part of the boat was decked over to make a small cabin and thus allow the boat to sail on longer trips, and they were also considerably deeper at the aft end of the keel than at the bow. This feature made a very handy vessel which could turn tightly – ideal for turning sharply to cast the ring-net in its characteristic circle. These popular and fast boats often took part in regattas.

During the early years of the twentieth century small petrol/paraffin engines were introduced for fishing boats. At a stroke boats could become independent of the wind and thus ensure the catch reached the market in good time. One of the first went into the skiff *Brothers* in 1907 when Robert Robertson of Campbeltown installed a Kelvin 7/9 horsepower petrol/paraffin engine.

Throughout his career Robert Robertson with his partners was to be at the forefront of innovation in ring-net boats. Experience gained with *Brothers* led him

8

Loch Fyne skiff 'Clan Gordon' UL240 in 1955. This boat became well-known for her prowess at the Clyde sailing regattas, and she was still sailing as a yacht in 1992.

W. G. McBride of Glasgow to develop a new design of motor ring-netter based upon boats he had seen in Norway. The first of these were *Falcon* and *Frigate Bird*, built by Miller of St Monans in 1921, and these pretty boats quickly revolutionised ring-netter design.

They were 50 feet (15.2 metres) long, fitted with two Gleniffer petrol/paraffin engines of 18/22 horsepower, and were completely decked over. A small pillar-box wheelhouse was provided for the helmsman. The most distinctive features, however, were the curving stem and the graceful shape of the canoe stern. These effectively allowed a big boat to have a relatively short keel length and so be able to turn tightly when shooting the ring-net.

Robertson's next effort at boat improvement was *Nil Desperandum* CN232, launched by Miller in 1928. This boat had the wheelhouse mounted forward

to provide a very large amount of clear working space for the net. This feature had also appeared on *Acacia* 133BRD of Kyleakin, Skye, in 1926, but it proved unsuccessful, not only because a wheelhouse in this position was uncomfortable in rough weather but because the skipper could not easily look behind at the net whilst steering in a tight circle.

The distinctive design of these ring-netters became the archetype for a large number of boats on both the east and west coasts. Generally post-war boats can be identified since they commonly have more buoyancy aft and a fuller-shaped cruiser-type stern. The introduction of more powerful winches and heavy engines enabled bigger nets to be used and accordingly the boats had to be modified to carry them.

This is one of the builder's photographs of the pioneer ring-netter 'Falcon' CN92 built by the famous yard of James N. Miller & Sons of St Monans in 1922 for the innovative Robert Robertson and John Short of Campbeltown. The rounded forefoot at the bow and the graceful curves of the canoe stern can easily be seen. Just visible forward of the bending figure is the pillar-box wheelhouse.

Left: *Ring-netter 'Nil Desperandum' CN232 on her builder's trials off St Monans in 1928. This revolutionary motor ring-netter was built by Miller in 1928 for John Short and Robert Robertson. She was one of the earliest boats to experiment with a forward wheelhouse in order to leave a large amount of clear deck space for working the net. On the foredeck is the little skylight over the crew's quarters.*

Right: *Many ring-netters regularly fished down to the Isle of Man. Here is 'Achates' LH232 in Peel harbour c.1955. As a second-generation boat she is broader than 'Nil Desperandum' and 'Falcon', and the curve of the canoe stern in its latter stages is fairly close to a straight line. The pride and care which went into these boats is exemplified by the beautifully varnished hull and wheelhouse.*

Left: *'Alliance' CN187 at Campbeltown in 1986. She was built at Girvan, Ayrshire, in 1974 as a dual-purpose ring-netter and trawler. The two gantries on each side towards the stern are the gallows which support the fairleads for the trawl warps, and mounted on a crane over the stern is the powerblock for hauling in the net. Note the larger wheelhouse and steel gantries replacing the wooden masts.*

'Gratitude' 207LH full to the brim with herring in Dunbar Harbour, c.1895. It was small undecked clinker-built skiffs such as this which were the backbone of the herring fleet in the first half of the nineteenth century. The single unstayed mast would carry the dipping lugsail, which can be seen lying with its yard on the left of the picture. The other poles lying on the fish are the oars.

THE GREAT EAST COAST LUGGERS

The Scottish east-coast fishing industry at the beginning of the nineteenth century was poised on the edge of rapid development. The government bounty for herring fishing had previously been paid for the building and equipping of large herring boats, but now this money was transferred to a bounty paid on each barrel of pickled herring produced. This was the incentive for fish curers to advance money to the small-scale fisherman for the purchase or fitting out of boats.

These were undecked double-ended clinker-built luggers which were cheap to build and could be rowed and sailed from an open beach. These small boats helped make efficient an industry which previously had been barely viable. This was clearly seen by 1830, when the bounty was abolished and the industry continued to thrive without government support.

As the century progressed the seasonal appearance of the herring shoals occurred gradually further out to sea and so boats had to become bigger in order to make the longer daily trips to catch them. A

Archie Smith in his small double-ended line-fishing skiff 'Janet' 412KY at Kinghorn, Fife, c.1890. He is wearing a full suit of oilskin waterproofs and a sou'wester. Clearly seen are the unshipped rudder lying on the thwart to his right and two oars and a mast. The oars would be worked from between the thole pins set into each top side of the boat, and the mast would be stepped on top of the keel and supported by the semicircular band visible on the aft side of the foremost thwart.

bigger boat can carry more nets and so catch more fish, which it can ferry more quickly back to shore. However, the open lugger was always restricted by the need to operate from a beach or small harbour with only as many nets as the crew could haul.

The character of boats in the first half of the century is captured in the official report by Captain Washington into the great disaster of 18th/19th August 1848 when 124 boats were lost and one hundred fishermen died. A fierce storm had caught the fleet by surprise and many boats and lives were lost owing to the inadequate nature of the harbours and the apparent unsuitability of the boats for the fishing they were now undertaking. The meticulous report seems to outline two general boat types amidst a large number of variations of shape and rig being used in each locality at that time.

The first type is the *scaffie*. These sailed mostly from beaches and harbours along the south coast of the Moray Firth and were characterised by a curved stem and forefoot and a very steeply raked stern. This made a relatively short keel and so allowed the boat to turn easily and be very manoeuvrable. By this time the keels were about 32 feet (9.75 metres) long but the overall lengths had reached 41 feet (12.5 metres), creating an overhang at the stern approaching 9 feet (2.75 metres). These boats often had two or sometimes three masts with lugsails and a crew of five, yet they were lightly built and weighed less than 3 tons so that they could easily be run up a beach.

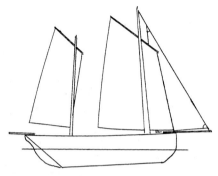

Scaffie, c.42 feet (12.5 metres).

The second boat type is known as the *fifie* and was found from Orkney to Berwick except in the southern Moray Firth, where the scaffie tended to predominate. The fifie was sharp and deep with a near-vertical stem and stern and a long straight keel. These powerful boats sailed well and fast, but they were not nearly as handy as the scaffies. The majority of them sailed

Fifie, c.70 feet (21.3 metres).

Boats described in Captain Washington's report.

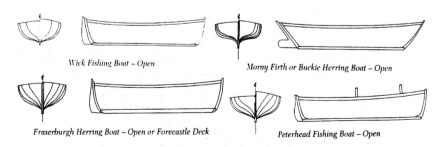

Wick Fishing Boat – Open

Moray Firth or Buckie Herring Boat – Open

Fraserburgh Herring Boat – Open or Forecastle Deck

Peterhead Fishing Boat – Open

Scaffies at Avoch Harbour, Inverness, c.1890. The distinctive shape of the scaffie is clearly seen in this photograph. The small boat in the centre foreground has the characteristic curved stem and steeply raking stern. Similar boats appear to be drawn up all along the beach in the background, although some may be small zulus. The big boat INS2121 on the right-hand side has the vertical stem and three beltings along the hull of a first-class zulu, and it is this boat that the children are keen to sit on.

with a dipping lug foresail set on a large unstayed mast and a standing lug on the mizzen mast. This simple rig left plenty of uncluttered space for hauling the nets but required great skill to handle safely in heavy weather. Safety on an undecked boat was helped by the weight always being low down, and the crew were less likely to fall overboard in rough weather. The fishermen also liked them because they could carry a great deal of fish. The Washington Report, however, is very critical and points out the danger of large undecked boats being swamped in bad weather.

The fishermen were in turn very critical of this section of the report, and partial decking of boats did not catch on for

Baldies lying in Newhaven Harbour, Edinburgh, c.1880. The overlapping clinker construction of the planks can be seen, but more particularly the forward half of each vessel is now decked in. Essentially these are larger half-decked versions of 'Gratitude'.

A forest of masts in Fraserburgh harbour, c.1890.

over a decade, when better-quality harbours allowed the much heavier-decked *baldies* to be worked. Named after Garibaldi, the hero of the Italian unification who was in the news during the 1860s, baldies were of fifie shape with the fore part decked over to provide a small cuddy for shelter.

The introduction of the baldie coincided with the development of the new cotton drift-net. These net sections weighed less than one-third of the weight of the older hemp nets and boats could carry many more sections, each linked together on a single rope and known as a 'fleet'. However, carrying home the extra fish caught

Dropping the foresail on fifie KY263 at the entrance to Pittenweem Harbour, Fife, 1895. Some idea can be gathered of the huge size of the rig in relation to the crewmen hauling it down, and of the high level of seamanship involved in sailing a big fifie. Without an engine or other assistance, the skipper is bringing his boat in at speed and dropping the sail at the last moment, hoping that the way on her will carry her to her berth. Note that the foresail has not been barked to preserve it and has yet to have its number painted. The practice was often to stretch a new sail by use for one season before barking it to a deep brown colour.

Clearing the drift-nets on a second-class fifie in Fraserburgh Harbour, c.1900. The crew are clearing the remaining herring from the meshes of the nets, watched by some local children. In the right foreground are the round floats or boughs which help support the nets in the water. The foresail is wrapped around its yard on the right and the end is hoisted up clear of where the men are working. The figure standing idly to the right is wearing leather seaboots and a guernsey or gansey top under canvas braces. The man with the sou'wester on the left is leaning against an 'ironman' hand-powered capstan with its large flywheel. Immediately behind him is the Peterhead fifie 'Cornucopia', where the boughs have been tied up to dry on the bowsprit, the far end of which is sitting in the crutch or mytch post for the mast when it is lowered. The boat in the background is a large first-class zulu with an INS registration, beneath which there are three wooden beltings around the hull.

required a bigger boat, which in turn could carry even more nets. In 1800 a boat might carry up to ten small nets in its fleet. By 1840 larger boats were carrying over twice as many, but by 1880 around fifty large nets might be carried, which represents a fourfold increase in catching power. Boat size was now limited by the amount of net that a crew could haul and by the maximum size of rig that a crew could handle. Only fully decked boats using carvel construction could be built to the scale required, and the introduction of a hand-powered flywheel winch or 'ironman' helped the crew to handle bigger rigs and more nets. Carvel construction consists of planks fastened on to a framework of ribs with the gaps between them filled by caulking to prevent leaks. Carvel boats are constructed skeleton first and the resultant boat is heavy but tough and long-lasting.

By 1900 these large-decked luggers

marked the peak in the development of the fifie and 70 feet (21 metres) long vessels fished with up to seventy nets each. These magnificent craft were very fast and powerful sailers in skilled hands, while the height of the rails was always restricted to 12 inches (30.5 cm), to allow the nets to be hauled in easily.

Among boatbuilders the appearance of a novel and innovative boat design is a rare event. Nevertheless in 1879 such a vessel appeared in the Moray Firth. The South African War was just drawing to a close and thus the new boat acquired its famous type-name – *zulu*. William Campbell of Lossiemouth built the first zulu, the appropriately named *Nonesuch*, by combining the tall vertical stem of the fifie with the deeply raking sternpost of the scaffie. The resulting hybrid proved to be one of the most striking and successful designs of British sail fishing boats and zulus were built in large numbers

15

Fifie LK828 with Shetland rig, c.1900. The men of Shetland, and sometimes those in the Moray Firth too, preferred the ketch rig to the dipping lugsail. This rig is handier in the enclosed waters around the voes and islands of Shetland. The near-vertical stem and stern of the fifie can clearly be seen, and she is sporting a large jib or spinnaker at the end of a long bowsprit. This was a essentially a sail for summertime and was common on the larger luggers too.

over the last two decades of the century. Only when it became apparent that the characteristic extreme rake to the stern was not easily adapted for the addition of a motor did new building markedly slow down.

The zulu was fast and weatherly and was quickly taken up by the men of the Moray Firth in place of the scaffie. By 1900 there were 480 zulus on the Buckie register alone. The vertical stem and deep forefoot held the bow well up to the wind and gave the zulu some of the sailing qualities of the fifie. The 45° rake of the stern made a

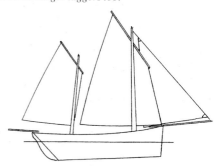

Zulu, c.80 feet (24.3 metres).

First-class zulu 'Research' LK62, formerly called 'Heather Bell', under restoration at St Monans. The distinctive vertical stem but steeply raking stern can be clearly discerned on this vessel.

A second-class INS-registered zulu dipping her foresail to tack in heavy weather, c.1900. The huge yard of the lugsail is being lowered and dipped around the rear of the mast before being hoisted up on the other side. This operation could take ten minutes and be extremely tricky in heavy weather.

short keel but a long waterline. Thus the vessel was easy to turn but had plenty of deck space, and the long waterline allowed higher speed when racing for the market.

By the early 1880s hand winches were being replaced by steam-powered capstans and these allowed the first-class fifies and zulus to grow to their ultimate size of around 80 feet (24.3 metres) long and 22 feet (6.7 metres) wide. The zulu *Laverock* BF787 of Hopeman, built in 1902, was reputedly the largest, at 84 feet (25 metres) long on a 59 foot (18 metre) keel with a 25 foot (7.6 metre) overhang! These fast craft with huge masts and sails became quite familiar along the whole of the east coast as they travelled down every year to the autumn herring fishery off East Anglia. Two to three hundred boats made this a regular practice in the 1860s, but by the end of the century over a thousand large Scottish luggers would join the English boats each year. Seven or eight men and a boy were now handling a string of seventy drift-nets on

Crew portrait of fifie 'Vanguard' KY603, c.1900. The crew might mark the end of a successful fishing season by having a portrait taken of themselves which could be sent as a postcard to family and friends. The crew of 'Vanguard' are dressed in oilskins and guernseys. Five men are sitting on the bowsprit. When a jib was being set, the bowsprit would be slid out forward through the circular gammon iron near the bow. Note the iron chain and hook to take the bottom of the foresail, the ropework fender beneath it, and the crutch or mytch post behind the man on the right which would take the lowered foremast when the vessel was lying to the drift nets.

There is continual danger at sea. Fifie 'Betty Inglis' ME165 lies with broken mast at Montrose Harbour in 1903. Two crewmen, Alex Pert ('Pickle') and Charlie Anderson, were killed when the foremast on this 53 foot (16.1 metre) fifie snapped in heavy weather at sea. The steam capstan and the foremast crutch or mytch post can clearly be seen by the mizzen mast. Note the half-open fish hold, the very low bulwarks with the heads of the frames protruding, and the small rail to protect the helmsman.

a rope over 2500 yards (2286 metres) long. They ate and slept in a small cabin in the stern. Their boat could set around 3650 square feet (339 square metres) of cotton canvas on the two masts. The foremast would be the same length as the keel, fashioned from a single Norwegian pine with a diameter at the deck of over 20 inches (51 cm), and the dipping lugsail on the foremast was slung from a 37 foot (11.2 metre) yard, which had to be lowered and dipped around the back of the mast each time the boat tacked.

Monument to a fifie at King's Lynn, Norfolk. This monument was erected for the crew of the St Monans fifie 'Beautiful Star' KY1298 by the people of King's Lynn. It is inscribed: 'Erected to the memory of eight Scottish fishermen drowned off the Norfolk coast in the November gale of 1875.' These were James Paterson, William Paterson, Robert Paterson, David Davidson, David Allan, Alexander Duncan, Thomas Lourie and Thomas Fayall.

Steam drifter 'North Briton' PD487 steaming from her home port, Peterhead, c.1910.

THE ADVENT OF STEAM FISHING

As the great sailing drifters were reaching their peak in around 1900, they were eclipsed by the successful application of steam propulsion to the drift-net fishing. Few large sailing boats were built in Scotland after 1903. The fishing fleets enjoyed almost unparalleled success between 1880 and 1914 and a steady growth in wealth encouraged investment in steam. A steam boat cost almost three times as much to build as her sailing equivalent and the expenses of coal and regular wages for the engineer and fireman were a significant fixed cost. The first two steamers to appear at Wick in 1880, the *Waterwitch* of Leith and the *Alpha* of Wick, although successful, were both offered for sale at the end of the season since they had failed to provide a sufficient return on the capital. Nevertheless the reward for this outlay was greatly enhanced catching power that was never subject to the fickle wind, and in the good years a steam drifter was a very profitable investment.

Steam had come to the drifter fleets later than among the trawlers. The power of the steam trawler allowed her easily to outfish an equivalent-sized sailing trawler and from the middle of the century a number of steam tugs had been converted to trawling, such as the Sunderland paddle tug *Messenger* in 1877. One of the pioneering purpose-built steam trawlers was *Thistle*, launched at Dartmouth in 1868, and over the last twenty years of the nineteenth century a great number of sailing trawlers were replaced with steamers.

The design of the steamers was based on the shape of the English East Anglian smacks. A straight stem on a long straight keel led aft to a graceful counter stern which, coupled with a high bow and a strong sheer, made a vessel which became famous for its seakeeping qualities. These early steamers had small compound steam engines and no wheelhouse, for they still retained a full sailing rig. The weight of boiler and engine required them to be sited towards the centre of the boat and

19

The early steam drifter 'Perseverance' LH3, c.1900, a 'Woodbine' steam drifter, so-called from the tall thin shape of a funnel that was always smoking. She has no wheelhouse and carries a full sailing rig. Built at Leith in 1886 for J. Willcock of Manchester, she had a 9 horsepower engine and was 67 feet (20.4 metres) long. Fifies sail in behind her. Sold to Yarmouth owners in 1914, she ended her days as a coal barge in Grimsby Docks in 1920.

Left: *Steam drifter 'Mare Vivimus' at Hartlepool in 1924. There is a Scots lass from Pittenweem in the wheelhouse, and on deck from left to right are E. Sutherland, an unknown local, Jess Horsburgh and Jimmy Anderson. The girls on deck are helping repair the drift nets.*

the tall thin funnels brought them the nickname of 'Woodbine' steamers. Increasing power and reliability of the engines allowed the sailing rig to be reduced and the comfort of a wheelhouse added, initially behind the funnel. The crew slept and ate in a cabin under the foredeck, the most uncomfortable part of the vessel. By the end of the century the layout crystallised into the steamer design which became a familiar sight in British ports for nearly fifty years. The wheel-house was placed amidships immediately in front of the funnel, behind which was a low deckhouse over the top of the engine room, leading to a small galley aft. The sailing rig was almost entirely removed. Drifters retained the respected steam capstan with the engine on its top, now positioned on the foredeck, while trawlers mounted a big trawling winch immediately in front of the wheelhouse.

In the early twentieth century the catching power of the steam drifter came to

Right: Steam trawlers in Granton Harbour, Edinburgh, c.1947. 'Madden' GN101 is in the foreground, and the larger boat 'Inchgarvie' GN30 lies behind. Immediately in front of 'Madden's' wheelhouse is the trawl winch and the hoop of the forward gallows for the trawl warp can be seen in line with her mast. Both vessels have enlarged wheelhouses and 'Inchgarvie' has a white whaleback shelter over her bow.

Left: Not every boat made it over the bar. A drifter wreck in the mouth of Yarmouth Harbour watched by a large crowd in 1906. Note the net boughs floating to the surface.

dominate the fish landings. In 1910 1200 Scots boats sailed to Great Yarmouth for the autumn herring season, about half being steamers. The steamers averaged a gross income of £530, while the sailing boats managed only £134. Nevertheless, the high fixed costs of the steamers meant that their net income was often much the same as that of the sailing drifters.

Such hard-working and seaworthy boats were ideal in wartime as minesweepers, tenders and patrol vessels, and many provided stalwart and heroic service in both world wars. 1249 steamers were taken up for the navy in the First World War, and these craft were returned after the war with the offer of a refit or a grant. A building programme to a standardised plan

Right: The steam drifter 'Spes Aurea' KY81 punching her way out of Yarmouth in October 1933. A Peterhead drifter is heading the other way. Note the mizzen sail used for steadying the drifter while lying to the nets.

An Admiralty standard steel steam drifter, 'Cosmea' KY21. 'Cosmea' was built by John Duthie of Aberdeen as standard drifter HMD 'Dusk' in 1918. She was 86 feet (26.2 metres) long with a 42 horsepower engine and was employed at various times as a liner, a drifter and a trawler. In 1951 her name was changed to 'Coriedalis' and in 1956 she had the distinction of being the last Scottish steam drifter to go to the East Anglian herring season.

was initiated to replace the boats which had been lost, and the new boats became known as Admiralty 'standard' drifters.

However, after the war the great markets for Scottish cured herring in Germany and Russia had collapsed completely, and with them went the viability of the steam drifter. As the price of herring crashed so the high costs of the drifter became crippling and a major depression in the fishing industry ensued for many years. Steam drifters were revealed as far less economic than the increasingly ubiquitous motor boats and very few were built after 1920. 437 went to war in 1939, but many were broken up after 1945 and by 1954 only six drifters were left in the Scottish fleet. It has been said that they broke many more hearts than ever they lifted.

Steam drifter 'Pilot Star' KY48 in the Firth of Forth in 1934. The steam capstan with its engine on top is prominent in the left foreground. The steam pipe from the boiler came up through the centre of the capstan. Note the bicycles on deck behind – is this a pleasure trip?

First-class motorised fifie 'Friends' FR983, c.1935. This venerable vessel was built by J. & G. Forbes of Fraserburgh as a large sailing fifie in 1903. In 1918 she was motorised and worked as a motor drifter until February 1951, when she was wrecked in Loch Linnhe. Note that she still retains her steam capstan, which is now mounted on the foredeck as in a steam drifter. Her sharp ends and narrow stern give away her origins as a purely sailing boat.

MECHANISATION AND THE MOTOR BOAT

The nostalgia that surrounds the passing of the age of sail and steam has sometimes deflected interest from the subsequent development of motor boats in Scotland. The number of motor boats overtook that of steam boats in 1915, and by 1920 there were 854 steamers, 1947 motor boats and around 4000 small sailing boats. It was the motor boat that caused the demise of the sailing fishing vessel, and where possible most sailing boats were converted to motor.

A fine example of a motorised first-class zulu is *Research* LK62, built as a sailing zulu in Banff in 1903. She was motorised after the First World War and thereafter successfully fished right through to 1968. She is now in the collection of the Scottish Fisheries Museum. Fifies with their near-vertical sternposts proved simpler to convert than zulus and until 1933 motor-powered fifies continued to be built. However, as motors became more powerful and more reliable, boat designs in-creasingly moved away from sailing-boat shapes to develop shapes more specific to their needs. The motor ring-netters had done this on the west coast, and the early seine-net motor boats on the Moray Firth made a similar break with tradition. John Campbell of Lossiemouth sold his uneconomic steam drifter/trawler in 1926 and replaced her with the motor boat *Marigold* INS234, a boat influenced by the round bow and stern of Danish seiners and probably the first purpose-built seiner in Scotland. A further revolution occurred in Fraserburgh in 1928 when *Cutty Sark* FR334 was launched as one of the first truly multi-purpose vessels. However, in 1930 the first successful big motor drifter, *Gleanaway* KY40, was built in a similar style to her steam-powered predecessors. The shape that proved so useful as a steamer provided a foundation too for the development of the larger motor boats during the Second World War and after.

War provided a further stimulus. 234

Motor fifie 'Onaway' KY278. 'Onaway' and her fellow 'Winaway' were launched in Fife in 1929 and became known as 'baldies'. They bore a slight resemblance to the smaller fifie types of that name from the 1860s, but these stoutly built fifies were always motor-powered. 'Onaway' was 53 feet (16.1 metres) long and she was designed to operate as a drifter or seiner. Although she looks like a sailing fifie, her stern is fuller and more buoyant to support a Gardner 48 horsepower semi-diesel engine. The crew's quarters were forward in the bow. These vessels were among the first in Scotland to be fitted with electricity to power the lights and radio, but note how she retains a steam capstan for drift netting.

'Gleanaway' KY40, at Yarmouth in 1931, was built for Provost Carstairs and J. Watson of Anstruther by J. & G. Forbes of Fraserburgh in 1930. She was one of the first successful big motor drifters and resembles a steam drifter of similar size except that she lacks a funnel and engine-room casing, and the rounded cruiser stern, which replaces the common counter stern on the steamers. 'Gleanaway' was eventually sold to South Africa, but one of her sisters was still fishing out of Penzance in 1991.

motor boats and 437 steamers were commandeered and twenty-nine sunk by enemy action. Over three hundred wooden patrol vessels were built with the intention that they could also be used as fishing vessels after the war. Eighty-five of these MFVs (motor fishing vessels or motor ferry vessels) were eventually bought in Scotland to replace some of the ageing steam drifters.

Since the end of the Second World War there has been a revolution as far-reaching as any previous one. The fishing boat has been dramatically transformed by the introduction of scientific construction and safety controls and of navigation and monitoring systems. The availability of grants and loans stimulated a post-war building boom of dual-purpose motor boats with tall raked bows and cruiser

Admiralty MFV number 324 'Craigewan' PD416. 'Craigewan' was built as a wartime MFV by Jones of Buckie in 1945. The boatyard in the background is that of Richard Irvin & Sons of Peterhead.

Hauling in a drift-net on board motor drifter 'Refleurir' KY16 in 1949. The net with the en-meshed fish is hauled in over an open roller. Notice the hand-painted 'scumbling' (the decorative wood-panelling effect) on the side of the wheelhouse.

Landing the catch from the traditional seine-netter 'Ocean Hunter II' at Pittenweem in 1973. The fish are being hoisted up from the hold in boxes. Note the many coils of the warps for the seine net. The winch in the centre has a coiler attached to ease greatly the work of hauling and coiling the warps.

sterns. These boats were often built from larch planks on oak frames, powered by Gardner or Kelvin engines, and their gear was hauled by Miller or Lossiemouth winches and Beccles coilers.

After 1960 restrictions on the smaller but high-powered foreign-built engines were lifted and one of the first Caterpillar engines was fitted into the ring-netter *Taeping* BA237 in Fraserburgh in 1964. The emphasis now turned to maximum power with maximum capacity and as a consequence boat shapes began to fill out. The fine bows and cruiser sterns made boats wet in bad weather and provided limited working space aft. The new boats

Strachans, accustomed to work in wild distant waters, had whaleback shelters over the bow from the 1950s. Since then the introduction of lightweight aluminium shelters has allowed first half the deck and then the whole of the forward deck area to be completely covered in on many boats. The crew are completely protected from the elements, and the effect of this big air pocket is to give the vessel an almost all-weather capability. Skippers can venture out and fish in weather that their predecessors would never have braved. The logical extension to the idea appeared in the late 1980s when shelter decks were fitted over the stern as well

The highly successful 'Silver Chord' KY124 in the early 1960s. 'Silver Chord' was built in Anstruther in 1956/7 to replace Skipper Muir's steam drifter 'Coriedalis' and immediately won him the annual Prunier Trophy for the largest haul of herring in one night during the East Anglian season.

are shorter, wider and rounder with broad 'Queen Mary' flared soft nose bows. They are designed simply to be working platforms able to carry big engines and big catches, and pretty shapes are sacrificed for efficiency. Although the cruiser stern remained popular until the 1970s, the truncated square stern now provides more working space aft, at the expense of speed and of manoeuvrabilty when going backwards.

Safety and comfort have been given a higher priority too. The large long-line or 'great-line' vessels, such as *Radiation* and

and the fishing gear is now worked through hatchways. One of the first with this design was *Sharona II* LH250, 75 feet long by 23 feet wide (22.8 by 7 metres).

A series of unexplained losses in the 1970s, such as the case of the Hull trawler *Gull*, led to tighter rules on boat designs. Yards were now finding that they could not readily do this work themselves and required the services of a naval architect. Stability tests were introduced for new boats too, and the minimum height of the bulwarks was raised.

Seine-netter/trawler 'St Kilda' INS47 at sea, c.1980. This round-sterned vessel was built in 1978 at Buckie for a successful Lossiemouth skipper. She not only has a whaleback shelter on her bow but also a half shelter deck over the crew working area in front of the wheelhouse. Note the large rope drums for the seine-net warps. These have replaced the traditional coilers on most seine-netters. The net itself is hauled with the aid of the powerblock mounted on the rear of the superstructure behind the mast. Immediately in line with it are the curved gallows on the side deck to carry the net warps. The five diagonal bands on the hull below the gallows are steel strengtheners which help protect the hull from the heavy metal trawl doors.

Wood did not become obsolescent as a boatbuilding material until the 1990s, when economic difficulties and the shortage of good boatbuilding timber combined nearly to put an end to its use. 80 feet (24 metres) long wooden-hulled vessels compete today in every way with their steel counterparts, and they could be cheaper to build and kinder to their fishing gear too.

Since 1992 emergency position-indicating radio beacons (EPIRB) have been required on all vessels. Safety has been further enhanced by the great leap forward in electronic systems, and wheelhouses have become bigger to accommodate the increasing array of equipment in use. From his wheelhouse chair the skipper knows exactly where he is, where his fishing gear is, and what and where the fish are. The improvements in navigation, communication and fishing equipment make

'Majestic' FR194 hauled out on the slip at Fraserburgh, c.1985. Note how very rounded and full the boat shape has become. Maximum capacity and power in a vessel are now the most important considerations for economically efficient operations.

The great liner 'Radiation' A115 leaving Lerwick after buying bait for her hooks in the mid 1960s. At 97 feet (29.5 metres) long, she is one of the largest wooden fishing boats built in Scotland and caused a sensation in the Fife ports. Notice the large aluminium wheelhouse with a radar scanner on the roof, and the skipper's cabin underneath. Note also the whaleback shelter over the bow, built to give some protection to the crew as they haul in the lines in the rough waters of the Iceland and Rockall grounds. As a great line vessel, her decks are relatively clear of the ropes and gear familiar on the drifters, seiners and trawlers. 'Radiation' is now in the collection of the Scottish Fisheries Museum.

'Crystal River' BCK16 in Lochinver in 1989. The powerblock and the gallows are quite distinct. 'Crystal River' was designed by MacAllister of Campbeltown and built in Buckie. She is powered by a 495 horsepower Caterpillar engine but the most distinctive feature is the filling in of the half shelter deck to make an entirely enclosed three-quarter shelter deck with only a side hatch and the stern from which to work the gear. The skipper in the wheelhouse now requires a closed-circuit television link to enable him to see the activity under the shelter deck.

28

The large purse-seiner 'Sedulous' FR228, c.1980. Loaded down to the gunwales with a huge catch of mackerel, 'Sedulous' is making her way up Loch Broom in order to sell her catch to the east European factory ships lying there. She is 133 feet (40.5 metres) long and powered by a 1000 horsepower engine. She was built in Norway in 1970.

further demands on power, often requiring boats to carry generator engines as powerful as those used as main engines in the 1950s. Hydraulics have replaced chain and belt drives for winches and allowed the full development of the powered net-hauler or 'powerblock', usually mounted aft on a hydraulic crane.

The very large purse-seiners are the chief successors to the herring drifters and ring-netters in the Scottish fleet. Technology has turned them into hugely efficient and merciless fishing machines. Locating the herring shoals by sonar, the purser can accurately cast the circular purse net around a volume of water the same size as a cathedral. It has been calculated that one purse-seiner with a crew of fifteen fishing for perhaps ninety days per year can outfish over five hundred boats of the 1840 fleet.

The traditional link between a boat's shape and its purpose has become less and less clear with time. Power and technology can override and transform the older familiar boat shapes, and as more versatile and efficient craft appear in order to cope with the swings of economic fortune their variety seems to decrease.

The large purse-seiner 'Challenge' FR77 working her purse-seine, c.1985. The ring of the purse-seine can clearly be seen on the water as the big purser winds it in.

Old-style ring-net skiffs on the beach at Dalintober, Campbeltown, Argyll. The very rounded stern of these skiffs is clear and suggests that they are probably from the middle of the nineteenth century.

GLOSSARY

Aft: towards the stern.

Bulwarks: side railings.

Canoe stern: a rising curved and pointed stern which does not curve back past the vertical.

Carvel: skeleton-first construction with planks lying next to each other.

Caulking: the material inserted between planks to stop leaks.

Clinker: shell-first construction with overlapping planks fastened to each other along their edges.

Dipping lug: a quadrilateral sail aligned with the centreline which must be dipped round the mast for each tack.

Double-ended: a boat pointed at both ends.

Drift-netting: method of herring fishing in which long stationary curtains of gill net are suspended vertically at night and in which free-swimming shoals become trapped.

Fireman: the crewman who stokes the fire for the steam boiler.

Frames: the structural ribs or skeleton of a carvel boat.

Freeboard: the distance between the water and the rail or deck edge.

Gunwale: the upper side edge of a boat (excluding the rail).

Long line: fishing method for white fish in which long lines with many baited hooks are laid along the seabed.

Lugsail: a quadrilateral sail aligned with the centreline and slung from a yard with its fore lower corner fastened down to the deck.

Mizzen: the rearmost mast or sail.

Purse-seine: fishing method in which a large circle net is cast, the bottom of which can be closed up like a purse, so trapping a shoal in a bag.

Ring-netting: fishing method in which a circle net is cast around a shoal and is then dragged sideways to trap the fish.

Saithe: a fish related to the cod.

Scarf: a joint used to make two long pieces of wood into one, typically used to connect the keel to the stem or sternpost.

Seine netting: fishing method in which a bag of net and its warps are set in a large triangle before hauling brings the sides together and the fish into the bag along the base.

Sheer: the longitudinal curve along the deck line of a vessel.

Skiff: an old European word for a boat.

Square sail: a quadrilateral sail set across the centreline of the boat and in front of the mast.

Standing lug: lugsail which is tied down in such a way as to obviate dipping the sail when tacking.

Stem: the leading edge of the bow.

Sternpost: the trailing edge of a vessel, upon which the rudder is usually hung.

Tack, tacking: the operation of turning about as a boat zigzags towards the direction of the wind.

Thole pins: upright supports against which the oars are worked.

Unstayed: a mast which stands on its own, free of supporting rigging.

Yole: a Norse word for a small boat.

SCOTTISH PORT REGISTRATION LETTERS

The registration letters used for Scottish registered fishing boats are tabulated here. Ports added to the list after 1887 are denoted by *; those added after 1892 are denoted by §, and those added after 1893 by †.

A	Aberdeen		INS	Inverness
AA	Alloa		K	Kirkwall
AD	Ardrossan		KL	Kirkwall
AG	Ardrishaig*		KY	Kirkcaldy
AH	Arbroath		LH	Leith
AR	Ayr		LK	Lerwick
BF	Banff		ME	Montrose
BO	Borrowstounness (Bo'ness)		ML	Methil†
BRD	Broadford*		OB	Oban*
BU	Burntisland†		PD	Peterhead
CN	Campbeltown		PEH	Perth
CY	Castlebay*		PGW	Port Glasgow
DE	Dundee		RO	Rothesay*
DS	Dumfries		SMH	St Margaret's Hope* (until 1889)
FR	Fraserburgh§		SR	Stranraer
GH	Grangemouth		SY	Stornoway
GK	Greenock		TN	Troon
GN	Granton		UL	Ullapool*
GW	Glasgow		WK	Wick
I	Inverness		WN	Wigtown
IE	Irvine†			

Peterhead packed with steam drifters, c.1910.

FURTHER READING

Gray, Malcolm. *The Fishing Industries of Scotland, 1790-1914.* Oxford University Press, 1978.

MacDonald, William. *Boats and Builders. The History of Boatbuilding around Fraserburgh.* Fraserburgh, 1993.

March, Edgar J. *Sailing Drifters.* Percival Marshall, London, 1952; reprinted by David & Charles, 1969.

Martin, Angus. *The Ring-net Fishermen.* John Donald, Edinburgh, 1981.

Sutherland, Iain. *From Herring to Seine Net Fishing on the East Coast of Scotland.* Camps Bookshop, Wick, undated.

Wilson, Gloria. *Scottish Fishing Craft.* Fishing News Books, 1965.

Wilson, Gloria. *More Scottish Fishing Craft and Their Work.* Fishing News Books, 1968.

Wilson, Gloria. *Scottish Fishing Boats.* Hutton Press, 1995.

PLACES TO VISIT

Intending visitors are advised to find out the times of opening before making a special journey.

Aberdeen Maritime Museum, Provost Ross's House, Shiprow, Aberdeen. Telephone: 01224 585788.

Arbroath Museum, Signal Tower, Ladyloan, Arbroath, Angus DD11 1PU. Telephone: 01241 875598.

Arbuthnot Museum, St Peter Street, Peterhead, Aberdeenshire AB42 6QD. Telephone: 01779 477778.

Eyemouth Museum, Auld Kirk, Market Place, Eyemouth, Berwickshire TD14 5HE. Telephone: 01890 750678.

Nairn Fishertown Museum, Laing Hall, King Street, Nairn IV12 4NZ. Telephone: 01667 456278.

Scottish Fisheries Museum, St Ayles, Harbourhead, Anstruther, Fife KY10 3AB. Telephone: 01333 310628.

Scottish Maritime Museum, Laird Forge Buildings, Gottries Road, Irvine, Ayrshire KA12 8QE. Telephone: 01294 278283.

Shetland Museum, Lower Hillhead, Lerwick, Shetland ZE1 0EL. Telephone: 01595 695057.

Wick Heritage Centre, 19/27 Bank Row, Wick, Caithness KW1 5EY. Telephone: 01955 5393.

An international context: the large herring trawler BF197 at Ullapool in 1980 is completely dwarfed by the huge Spanish freezer trawler lying behind her.